Also By Christine E. Ray

Composition of a Woman

<u>Anthologies</u>
Swear to Me (Gagnier)

Anthology Volume I: Writings from the Sudden Denouement Literary Collective (Editors: Kerkau, Austin, &Ray)

We Will Not Be Silenced: The Lived Experience of Sexual Harassment and Sexual Assault Told Powerfully Through Poetry, Prose, Essay, and Art (Editors: Ray, Austin, Daquin, & Finch)

All The Lonely People (Gagnier)

Praise for *The Myths of Girlhood*

Ray brings back my love of poetry, she throws it into an empty room and it proliferates, sometimes frighteningly, until it's half way down my throat and I only want more. A once in a life time author will cause you to become obsessive, you'll never truly get enough, and you'll forget your other lovers. That's how I feel upon reading Ray's work and I am certain of one thing, she's only going to keep surprising us, because despite everything, she lives for her art, and it shows, in the sheer force of her will to write it out, and touch us with her fire. She alone can create a cage, set a stage for madness, tattoo a feeling, gut an emotion or twist my psyche with an uncanny awareness of what makes us tick. If we know everything then the only thing left is what we make of the fall out, and Ray is the mistress of revealing what lies beneath us.

-Candice Louisa Daquin, *Pinch the Lock*

In 'The Myths Of Girlhood', Christine Ray has pulled her voice and her strength from her debut collection, 'Composition of a Woman' and she has pushed the status quo once again, writing hard truths into beautiful lines, she has asked you to make a choice: should you stay and placate society, leave your young girls to fend for themselves, throw them to the wolves or bring them, guilt and strength, wearing the pride of their mothers into this time.

'The Myths Of Girlhood' lays out the lies we have fed to our daughters, the pain we have all had to swallow, and the promises we have yet to fulfill. But with this work Christine Ray is paving the way for us all, showing us how to shed the shame and the vulnerability that we have worn for far too long.

-Nicole Lyons, *Blossom and Bone*

Through her use of strong, stark imagery we look in the mirror with the poet and face ourselves and all the monsters who maimed, the demons we've survived, and the dragon who longs to burst out of her self-actualized breast to embrace her freedom.

Ray's elegant poetry tells us 3D stories of a real woman's life. We root for our hero as she tears off layers. Grows into herself. Names herself; poet, boss, lover, mother, SURVIVOR and with a small, two-word line as loud as a thunder-clap, "my own."

-Rachael Ikins, *Just Two Girls*

Praise for *Composition of a Woman*
Christine E. Ray' debut book of poetry and prose

Christine Ray's debut collection *Composition of a Woman* is an extraordinary glimpse into the essence of what it takes to make, and sometimes simultaneously break, a woman as strikingly powerful as she is beautiful. . .

Christine Ray holds nothing back when she writes about the pain of depression and a failing body. She is raw and unashamed when she speaks to sexuality and the way society still reeks of misogyny and the absence of humanity. But at her very best she is empowering, speaking to the brave and reckless women who she lovingly refers to as sisters.

Composition is a beautiful book that takes the time to acknowledge that while some of the weight we carry through life may not be ours to carry, sometimes carrying it is just as important as knowing when to let it all go.

-Nicole Lyons, *Blossom and Bone*

Poet Christine Ray's first printed collection of poetry, *Composition of a Woman* (Sudden Denouement Press, 2018) is a striking, fearless foray into the psyche of womanhood, both highly relatable and intensely personal for female readers and achingly candid and fascinating for male."

-Candice Louisa Daquin, *Pinch the Lock*

In poems strung together like delicate bones, Ray has crafted a personal story that sometimes hinges on the idea of betrayal, but also on the inner strength of a woman finding love even as she has found loss, finding her voice in spite of being told she is less than. The trajectory follows an atlas of human form, from nerve to blood, in which she describes a relationship to her body, to her thoughts, to her womanhood, to her writer's existence. I was taken in (admittedly in part by my own fondness for the poetics of muscle and bone) from the first poem, by words and phrasing that hang on themselves gracefully in their simplicity while conveying a multitude of emotions.

The imperative of a poet is often to unveil some hidden kernel of human nature or experience and attempt to imbue it with feelings that are difficult to translate into words. To be an interpreter whose words reassure the readers that every experience is exquisitely unique and yet relatable. In this, Ray succeeds. . .

-Mariah Voutilainen, *Indie Blu(e)*

The Myths Of Girlhood
Christine E. Ray

The Myths of Girlhood
Copyright © 2019 Christine E. Ray

All rights reserved.
Printed in the United States of America.
No part of this book may be used, stored in a system retrieval system, or transmitted, in any form or in any means – by electronic, mechanical, photocopying, recording, or reproduced in any manner whatsoever - without written permission from the author, except in the case of brief quotations embodied in critical articles and reviews.

For information, address Indie Blu(e) Publishing.
indieblucollective@gmail.com

Published in the United States of America by Indie Blu(e) Publishing

ISBN 978-1-7328000-1-4
Library of Congress Control Number: 2019900264

Editor: Kindra M. Austin
Cover Design: Mitch Green

Dedication

To my warrior sisters and brothers in survival who own their truth with such stunning courage and conviction. You truly transform your blood into ink.

x

Acknowledgements

Dennis Earley- Thank you for plodding through version after version of my original opus and convincing me that it needed to become two books. Your instincts were spot-on my friend, as was your title suggestion, *The Myths of Girlhood*. I hope the finished book is as badass as you believed it could become.

Georgia Park, Kristiana Reed, and Nicholas Gagnier- Thank you my dear beta readers for so generously providing the gifts of your time, wisdom, keen eyes, and unflagging support. *Myths* is a much better book because of you.

Candice Louisa Daquin, Rachael Ikins, and Nicole Lyons- I am so humbled that you read and reviewed the advanced copy of *The Myths of Girlhood*. You are forces to be reckoned with in the poetry universe and your support and encouragement means the world.

Stephen Fuller- Yes, we really did write *Night Rolls Over* together all those months ago! Thank you for allowing it to appear as part of this collection. You are wicked awesome my friend, and a pretty damn good writer yourself.

Mitch Green- I could not love this cover any more than I do. Thank you for letting me wrap your brilliant artwork around my words.

My *Blood Into Ink* and *Whisper and the Roar* sisters and brothers- Thank you for always believing in me. You make me brave.

Kindra M. Austin- You are the best partner-in-crime and editor a poet could ever have. Thank you for being Spock to my Kirk and for always having my back.

To Kevin, Elijah and Al- Thank you for keeping a roof over my head, dinner on the table, listening to me babble, making me laugh and ensuring that I am never bored. I love you dearly and am grateful for you every day.

Table of Contents

Dedication ix
Acknowledgements xi
Table of Contents xiii
Queen of Nothing 17
Black and Blue 18
A Room So Still and Quiet 19
Dissolution 20
My Beast 21
I Cast A Shadow 22
Illusions of Grandeur 23
Flight of Icarus 24
Sweet, Sweet Madness 25
Go Ask Alice 26
Wonderland 28
Wrecking Ball 29
You Are What You Eat 30
Tightrope 31
Self-Inflicted 32
What Remains 33
Night Rolls Over 34
Child Welfare 35
Truth 38
Breathe Out In Black 39

Nautilus	40
Survivor's Guilt	41
Lattice	43
Backside of the Night	44
The Charges Leveled	45
I Choke on Breath and Bone	46
Where My Ghosts Come Out to Play	48
The Charges Leveled	50
Muscle Memory	51
Trigger Finger	53
Unforgotten	54
Devout	55
Blue Moon	57
Second Star to the Right, Straight on 'til Morning	58
My Dear Companion	60
Cats Eye	62
Dangerous Beauty	63
White Flag	64
Undone	66
Ivory Brushed With Starlight	67
The Jewels in My Throat	69
Brave Enough	70
Feline	71
What's Your Poison?	72
Confessional	74
Depleted	76

Cat's Tail	77
Cold Bone and Ash	78
Point of Impact	79
Unrepentant	80
Choke Hold	82
Black Widow	83
A Righteous End	84
Shoes (Charlottesville, Virginia)	86
Magical Thinking	87
The Name They Call Her	88
Young Wolf	90
Strident	92
Ode to a Black Eye	93
Myths Of Girlhood	96
Made For Him	98
Objectification	99
Stone Angel	101
I Knew My Name	103
Adam's Rib	105
Jesus Died for Somebody's Sins	106
Wire in the Blood	108
My Sins	110
The Skin I'm In	112
The Monsters Under My Bed	113
Wolves	117
What Lies Beneath	118

The Choices Before Me	120
The Alchemist	122
That Which Was Awoken	123
This Room Is Not For Rent	124
I Ain't No Damsel	126
Resurrection	128
The Gifts I Am Given	130
Garden Bed	132
Gems	133
There Will Be Dragons	135
Nightingale	138
Poetry	139
Our Blood into Ink	140
Introductions	141
About the Author	145
About Stephen Fuller	147

Queen of Nothing

I sat in cherry
upon the hand carved
throne of ivory
in an empty room
of chiseled stone
its vaulted ceilings
echoed with silence
black and white diamond tiles
patterning the floor
no woven tapestries
of virgins fair
or unicorns
softened the harsh space
the cold bitter chill
seeped into my bones
my breath an icy mist
frost licked at the
leaded windows
of this frozen dream
no servants to wait upon my word
no court held in my thrall
queen of nothing
of no one
not even myself
to command
I long to return to a
richer sanity

Black and Blue

sprawled on the floor
staring sightlessly
at the ceiling
uncomfortable on
unrelenting surface
too inert to move
doesn't matter
where my body lies
trapped in my head
haunting myself
my own ghost
of remorse

A Room So Still and Quiet

a room so still and silent
that it hurts
stark white walls
razor sharp edges
etch my soul
draw blood
that drips
slowly
soundlessly
from my mouth
I am
a fly in amber
time stands still
air is thick
viscous
holds me motionless
in this prison cell
vibration of a
silent scream ringing
from my depths

Dissolution

words
some days my savior
some days my hell
dissolve
into
fragmented syllables
lonely letters
that I cannot
reassemble
back
into meaningful
wholes
I lie
tell myself
I will grow accustomed
to this silence
these padded walls

My Beast

caged beast
hidden in my breast
screams inchoate rage
beats its fists
bloody pulp
against metal ribs
until they splinter
reunited
we cling fiercely together
curl in the corner
rocking rapid
hiccupping rhythms
we don't cry pretty
we teeter on the edge of madness
wonder why
we are
never
enough

I Cast A Shadow

in lost hours
dim rooms
I silently mold
my hands
in front of
bare bulbs
project distorted
shadow puppets
against
lonely walls
movement
slow
inelegant
a mourning dove
pierced through
the breast
by melancholy's
sharp sterling thorn
beats its wings
ragged
against ribbed
cage
of blue
unable to
launch
fly free

Illusions of Grandeur

scrubbed free of pretense
my face
my soul
left raw
naked
fine lines radiate out
create delicate starburst pattern
like stone hitting thin ice
bullet penetrating glass
illusion of integrity maintained
until the lightest touch
in the most vulnerable place
shatters me into beautiful shards
that refract prism colored light
onto cold
white
walls

Flight of Icarus

there is an unexpected beauty
to the unraveling
freedom
in becoming
boneless
shapeless
unmoored
untethered
to here
to now
feels like my soul
could explode
out of my chest
in an explosion of light
could fly
could soar
reach for the heavens
the sun
like Icarus
before wax melts
and I return to
tumbling freefall
praying to lose consciousness
before I slam
broken
into the ground

Sweet, Sweet Madness

I splintered today
like a sheet
of spun sugar
smooth
glossy
transparent
my reality punctured by
sharp candy
as it shattered on my lips
sweet to my tongue
as it drew blood
in the soft recesses
of my mouth
I accepted my medicine
swallowed shards whole
they traveled downward
penetrated the walls
of my chest
embedded themselves deeply
into my heart
stained glass knives honed like razors
able to slice through
old wounds
ribboned scars

Go Ask Alice

prescription bottles
stand at attention
upon the kitchen table
we arm wrestle for control
of my identity
meaningless
that I am the one
who made the call
acknowledging my unraveling
I did not want
mini-pharmacy
growing unrestrained
blue pill to make me tall
red pill to make me small
stagger under weight of
laden words
found
in the psychiatric index
well- meaning shrink
in his trendy suit
sharp thin tie
shaggy Beatles cut
groovy glasses
tells me it does not matter
what we call
my crazy
as long as the pills
do the trick
he is talking
treatment implications
while I picture
strings of letters
carved into my forehead

with a dull knife
labeling my psyche
a Viennese Sorting Hat
with a cigar
declaring my diagnosis loudly
to room of my peers
shouting that neither
the Bipolar ones
nor the Bipolar twos
get to live in
Gryffindor Tower
before asking me
how I really feel
about my father

Wonderland

barely breathing
heartbeat slowed
blood moving sluggishly
through ambivalent veins
my only detectable
signs of life

mirage
on the horizon
hallucination
that I am looking
at you
looking at me
your expression
inscrutable

mirror
on the wall
cannot be trusted
no truth to be found
in my own reflection

perhaps I am meant instead
to step through
this looking glass
fall down the rabbit hole
surrender to the madness
become the red queen

Wrecking Ball

I watched from outside myself
as I took the wrecking ball
with hands that were my hands
and not my hands
swung it high above my head
demolished
what I held dear
surprised that the hands
that were mine but weren't mine
held such strength
most days things slide
through them
as though they are boneless
I looked at the rubble remaining
remembering how deeply self-hatred
can run
and how much collateral damage
is left in its wake

You Are What You Eat

I do not remember
who I used to be
how *she* used to feel
only know
that this stripped down woman
who currently inhabits my skin
like a suit
has been dining on pain
like a delicacy
spitting out kindness
empathy
like watermelon seeds
self-hatred rendering gentler fruit
indigestible
to my system

Tightrope

barefoot
I stand on the tightrope
of vulnerability
over a roiling pit
never knowing
if it contains acid
that will dissolve my skin on contact
or honey
that could coat my tongue
ease my aching soul
no pebbles to toss
to test my theories
I fight for balance
before succumbing
to old habits
cut myself to the bone
with sharp steel
wondering
if the drops of blood
will attract butterflies
or sharks

Self-Inflicted

the wounds
I inflict on myself
are administered
with surgical precision
using sharp knife
of bitter self-recrimination
on long, dark nights
of the soul
I am capable of
carving hundreds
of tiny cuts
on my heart
my psyche
if guilt
and worthlessness
are overwhelming enough
I will pour
orange juice on them
for good measure
leaving me sticky
seeping blood
and citrus
reassured for the moment
by exquisite pain
biting through the numbness
that I am still alive
still have substance

What Remains

the man-made chemicals
that surge through my blood
bind firmly to neurotransmitters
& smooth rough edges
erase a little more of me
each day
joy dissolves a fragrant mist
into the air I exhale
sadness a gentle stream of water
running harmlessly
between my fingers
but the rage?
the rage
always
remains

Night Rolls Over
Stephen Fuller and Christine E. Ray

this still, lonely hour
removes our masks
strips us to bone and shadow.
angels dance naked
on moonlight laughing
underneath waterfalls.
cold water drips
from goose pimples
invoking hidden gods within us
we grab hold of a wing
rip a feather from its rib
and dip it into the falls
let icy ribbons ink our skin
carve new features
into the alabaster face
we focus moonlight
on dried skins
and let them catch fire
the flames that singe
into our naked shadow
dance like holy spirit inside
our night rolls over
onto its backside
holding down the day

Child Welfare

I am in my child welfare class in graduate school
the room is full
class starts at 4 pm
it is dim
warm
my classmates and I are drowsy
longing for a snack
some caffeine
unexpectedly
the professor puts on a film
a surprisingly graphic film
about child sexual abuse
I am fine
I am fine
I am fine
I am *not* fine
I am rushing out of the classroom
heart thudding
hands shaking
I make it to the restroom
The privacy of the stall
before I vomit copiously
into the white porcelain bowl
knees sore on cracked
black and white checkerboard tile
I have never used the words
sexual abuse
in relation to myself
but my body is telling me
a different narrative
I have had lovers
who are sexual abuse survivors
I have always told myself

that what happened to *me*
was not like
what happened to them
I told myself
that floating on the ceiling compiling my grocery list in my head
while having sex
was *normal*
that my constant need for control
was *normal*
that my inability to let anyone touch me while vulnerable
was *normal*
that feeling nauseous while looking at pictures of myself
from elementary school
was *normal*
that wanting to die at 12 years old
was *normal*
as I fight my panic in the bathroom
praying that no one else
will need to use it
I am finally forced to admit to myself
that I am feeling
anything but *normal*
I am surprisingly
unnerved
as though I have never seen
the young woman
looking back at me
in the mirror
it takes some time
to regulate my heartbeat
calm my breathing
splash cold water on my face
school my expression into something
cool

neutral
before returning to class
to watch the rest
of that damn film

Truth

truth is a tangled rope
as thick as her wrist
studded with thorns
shards of broken mirror
pearls
sprigs of fragrant salvia
slippery with blood
and memory

Breathe Out In Black

wandering long
stark
white hallways
of the maze
in my mind
that I have rendered
featureless
sterile
scrubbed clean with sand
until it sparkles
until it bleeds
I have inhaled all the memory
all the chaos
the pain
deeply into my lungs
in an effort to purify it
bronchi of sage and charcoal
I breathe out in black
a thick cloud of smoke
that floats in the air
leaving me empty
momentarily pure
weightless

Nautilus

I travel the spiral path
bare feet sinking deep
into soft sand
circles twisting ever tighter
as I navigate this nautilus
walls curved and translucent
smooth to outstretched fingers
ceiling growing ever towards me
as I descend through chambers
of memory
become lost in smell of beach plum
bayberry
salt air
call of gulls
long stretches of beach
walked alone at sunrise
after slipping out
of the house of sorrows
rendered a ghost
invisible to distracted adults
vulnerable girl child
lost to view
drowning silently
in treacherous seas

Survivor's Guilt

time is slipping away from me
minutes
hours
lost
not complete blanks
but blurs
periods of fuzzy memory
gaps that I can't *quite* fill
my therapist brain dispassionately
tells me
that I have been dissociating again
disappearing from my own life
my grip on myself
on reality
increasingly tenuous
part of me is deeply concerned
part of me is professionally fascinated
wants to keep case notes
as I disintegrate
the past is breathing down my neck
like a shadowy beast with foul breath
its acid saliva
dripping down
my bare shoulder
burning my skin
refusing to be ignored
no intention
of going back into the lock box
as I unravel
I do what I do best
I talk around what is
consuming my thoughts
take a bubble bath

in my self-hatred
turning the water pink
blaming myself
hating myself
is so much easier for me to swallow
than the helplessness
the vulnerability

Lattice

I come back to myself this morning
find that I am staring at wallpaper
unconsciously tracing geometric patterns
with my fingertip
over and over
I am not the strong blue lines
that intersect
I am the empty white spaces
in the center of the hexagons
I am the void

Backside of the Night

haunted hours
when my ghosts emerge
from the ether
waltz in slow rotation
through my memory
music only they can hear
played by a skeletal orchestra
backside of the night
when my demons
come out to play
leapfrog through
my dreams
like rowdy children
with fangs
with talons
red rover
red rover
shall we play
hide and seek?

The Charges Leveled

they charged me with my sins
real and
imagined
sentenced me to a lifetime
of solitary confinement
in memory
handed me the knife of remorse
wickedly sharp
mirrored surface reflecting
my innocence lost
on an endless loop
and then told me not to bleed
on their clean floor

I Choke on Breath and Bone

world spinning
out of control
I am the center
of a tornado
called *flashback*
sharp fingernails dig
into tender palms
leave angry red ovals
in my flesh
pain is grounding
when I
can control it
focus on my breathe
deep inhale in
to count of five
slow exhale out
to count of ten
I run out of air
gasping
the knot of memory
is sharp as a chicken bone
as it gags past my windpipe
wedges in the roof of my mouth
I worry at it
with my tongue
as if it is a stubborn baby tooth
hanging by single thread
there is sharp pain
metallic taste of blood
as I finally dislodge it
spit it on the floor
an enormous black moth
feathered wings wet

with blood
and saliva
dazed on the floor
before I can catch it
it flies wobbly away
still holding my secrets
my nightmares
in its hollow silver belly

Where My Ghosts Come Out to Play

the room is tastefully decorated
respectful distance kept
between her desk
near the door
and the comfortable chair
I selected the first time
we met
now unanimously understood
as mine
my arms fold tightly
across my chest
hands unconscious fists
small table next to me
holds Kush balls
and engraved stones
with reassuring words like *hope* and *peace*
and a box of tissues
that I do not like
to need
art on the walls is soothing colors
mostly abstract compositions
except for the print of colorful umbrellas that rests
on the floor against the small filing cabinet
this is my favorite
she keeps the office lights low
I watch the dust motes dance
in the weak sunbeams
in the open space between us
'where do we start talking about the trauma?'
asks the kind voice across the room
the tightly barred door
that swings slowly open on rusty hinges
making a loud noise of protest

is the door labeled *loss*
my ghosts start to emerge
from that cavernous space
one by one
until the room is full of transparent shapes
curious to find themselves exposed to the light
'how does it feel to talk about this with emotion?'
without your usual detachment
not as if you are reporting the news?'
'it fucking hurts' I think sarcastically to myself
snapping the rubber band
she has given me to help stay grounded
harder and harder
against the tender skin
of my wrist
and then force myself to stop
under her concerned eye
reminding myself
that I really do *not* want to keep
hurting myself
being my own worst enemy
inflicting my own wounds

The Charges Leveled

they charged me with my sins
real and
imagined
sentenced me to a lifetime
of solitary confinement
in memory
handed me the knife of remorse
wickedly sharp
mirrored surface reflecting
my innocence lost
on an endless loop
and then told me not to bleed
on their clean floor

Muscle Memory

suddenly unsettled
when healing hands
touch
left side of
bare abdomen
images of stray cocks
and
cocked guns
fill my head
crowding out other
more mundane thoughts
unsure if these
moving pictures
that shrink me down
to size
belong to me
bear my childhood initials
buried memories
floating to the surface
from released fascia
or if they are a montage
of every photo
every movie
I have ever seen
about exploited children
is it more reassuring
to think myself
merely suggestible?
breathing through it
I resist the overwhelming urge
to cover my vulnerability
with my hands
wait for pulse to slow

nausea to pass
jaw to unclench
betrayed again
by my own body
my own weak flesh

Trigger Finger

soft hand
in velvet glove
holding
still smoking gun
that triggered me
did not mean harm
and yet . . .
the hole
in my gut
leaks blood
dark crimson
that spreads
like spilled ink
it was a clean shot
through and through
that caught me unaware
crushed bone and
memory
created the outline
of my body
on hard cement floor
ignore the scene
of the crime
I am deft
at resurrecting
mopping
the mess

Unforgotten

elliptical movement
of Mars' orbit
partially eclipsed
the memories
from view
but Phobos
Deimos
shine bright tonight
in the tight fold
of marble arms
across my chest
taste of bitter bile
that eats at the back of my throat
fierce clench of my glass jaw
refracting crimson light
of twin moons
I feel your shade wake, stir
pull at the phantom threads that
once bound us
I am momentarily undone
to discover you
unforgotten
by nerves beneath my skin
but experience has taught me
that you too will burn off
like tendrils of grasping fog
with the arrival of
the dawn

Devout

I have worn my armor
so devoutly
buckled on thick titanium plates
donned my Templar helm
until only eyes
and mouth
were visible
let this armor become my prison
a soldier in silent battle
on an empty field

I have treated
protecting
my vulnerability
my hidden depths
like a religion
something holy
something sacred
a duty requiring
constant vigilance

I have stood
locked in place
sweat dripping down my back
the heft
weight
of my protection
folding me in half
diminishing me
muffling everything
everyone
not contained in this suit of arms
this shiny sarcophagus

weary of the battle
but full of trepidation
fingers trembling
clumsy
I start to slowly remove
the pieces
let them fall to my feet
like abandoned dogma
rediscover the feel
of sunbaked hair
cool spring breeze against
warm skin
feel of flesh
grasping my hand
the piercing ice water pain
of awakening heart
that reminds me that I breathe
that I bleed
pure red rivulets
down pale skin
remember what it is like
to be
painfully
achingly
alive

Blue Moon

I fear that my heart
is the moon
full of cold silver light
mysterious and ancient
too large to hold in your arms
always just a little out of reach

Second Star to the Right, Straight on 'til Morning

he found her under the porch
where animals hide
to lick their wounds alone
heartbeats racing
bodies trembling
tears trailing
down faces
covered in dirt
from the dark
dusty recesses
it's not clear
what impulse
made him
extend a hand
she *looked*
like she might bite
but he was good-hearted
and knew a thing
or two
about days
like today
that drive children
to hide
under porches
it's not clear
what impulse
made her
accept the hand
he had a kindness
in his eyes
and she was brave

even when scared
cautiously she emerged
squinting into the sun
the open ground felt
vast
exposed
vulnerable
they quickly negotiated
climbing into
the wide boughs
of the oldest oak
where they sat for hours
eating apples
talking about
pirate ships
that sail in the clouds
treasure troves
and the best stars
to navigate by

My Dear Companion

we have only recently met
but there is a sense
of inexplicable connection
an easiness of souls
like greeting an old, dear friend
whom I have a long
history with
as if we had shared
a babysitter as toddlers
and peanut butter sandwiches and Fritos
in the lunchroom in second grade
protected each other
from classmates' hurtful words
fought off each other's bullies
on the playground
provided Band-Aids for
each other's first broken hearts
what is it about you
that feels so comfortable?
so much like home?
there is a piece of you
that feels like
it could be a piece of me
kindred spirits, twin souls
I am struck by the fact
that your bright shining soul
is easy to embrace and love
unconditionally
even from afar
if I can feel that tenderness
for your heart
for your soul
that feels at times

as familiar as my own
my new-old friend
could I learn to love
that piece of me?

Cats Eye

Your words roll toward me
across the table
like cats eye marbles
that I can pick up and examine
wonder at the jewel toned beauty
the sculptured moments captured inside
the delicate swirl
drawing me closer
defenses forgotten as I contemplate
the gifts offered
love
friendship
loyalty
respect
trust
intimacy
hope
encased in glass
awaiting my need
should I choose
to stow these precious orbs
in a soft pouch
hanging around my neck
falling close to my heart

Dangerous Beauty

I reach
for the dangerous beauty
you hold in your eyes
I know
that those eyes
that honey mouth
with its silver tongue
make all kinds of promises
that you might deliver on
or not
depending on your mood
or whether Mercury is in retrograde
or whatever coin you like to flip
heads you win
tails
I lose anyway
I suspect
but the look you are giving me right now
the way it makes me feel
makes me think it may be worth
the trip to hell

White Flag

your mouth is so close
that I can feel
the warmth
of your breath
smell your last
cup of coffee

we have been circling
each other
for weeks
darting closer
drawing back
unsure of
each other's signals

the uncertainty
makes me crazy
unable to decide
whether to pull you in
or shove you away

we look like
the two dancers
we saw on stage in Boston
last summer
a lithe, trembling
pas de deux

your scent is in my nose
if you linger here
any longer
motionless
I may bite

draw blood

it is exquisite
torture
this push-pull
between us
molten electricity

the silver cord
connecting us
at times elastic
at times steel
keeps us firmly
in each other's orbit

I feel like
I might die
if you touch me
and I will
most certainly die
if you do not

are we negotiating
consent
a truce
or surrender?

Undone

my quiet stretches out
a web of shadow
words unsaid
black diamonds
glittering on delicate strands of moonlight
that shine through frosted windows
I kneel
naked
vulnerable
in the shade cast by candle flame
I am undone
brought low
I have no language
to express need
no words
to beg for comfort
only silent tears
averted eyes
aching heart
weary head
clenched fists
to hide the shaking
have you learned me
enough
to understand
that tonight
the first move is yours to make
that you must be the strong one?

Ivory Brushed With Starlight

are you angel
or demon
man with ivory wings
brushed with starlight?
you are still
silent
but your ancient eyes say
that you have seen the color
of my soul
have studied it contours

your nostrils flare slightly
scenting my blood in the air
you see the crisscrosses
carved deep on my palms
at your knowing look
the knife in my hand drops
from suddenly nerveless fingers
blood wells from the cuts
dripping to the ground
consecrating the earth
you gently capture my wrists
cup my hands in yours
golden tears drop from your
otherworldly eyes
falling onto my damaged skin
transfixed I watch your sorrow
heal my wounds

you release my hands
cup my face reverently
your kiss is honey and cardamom
I am filled with your light

as your soul expands
to fill all my damaged places
I understand suddenly
that my heart
matters to you
and I am transformed

The Jewels in My Throat

longing has crystallized
in my throat
hard blue star sapphires
multi-faceted rubies
tear shaped diamonds
ropes of pearls
that threaten to choke me
riches I cannot spend
blood gems
polished by the fire in my belly
passion and rage
that always leaves me hungry
hollow
always wanting
more

Brave Enough

are you brave enough
to love the suicide girl
pierced with silver
dressed in black ink
whose vanity
was shorn off with her hair?
are you strong enough to drive away
the wolves who worry her door?
can your words drown out
their mournful howls
calling out to her feral heart?
are you ready for the demons
who come with black roses
during long dark nights of her soul
whispering their ugly lies
poking her deepest fears with their dirty nails
wooing her to the razor sharp edge?
or are you just another would-be lover
who tasted death on her tongue
the blood in her tears
and ran?

Feline

We never talked about the monster inside me. Crouched on the bed, cold white skin, dark pupils dilated like dinner plates, your bodily fluids fragrant on my tongue, feral and remote, licking my own blood off my fingers. Repulsive and enticing in equal turns. Never knowing if I would fade into the night for days or months, or pounce like a panther, holding you hostage on the edge of pain and pleasure, making you moan deep in your throat, your fingers knotted in wrinkled sheets, relishing your scream of release that I alone owned, finally settling down like a contented house cat, licking cream off both our mouths.

What's Your Poison?

some of us spent our 20's
lost in the bottle
some popped pills
stuck a needle in our arm
drove 100 miles an hour
took crazy risks
there are those of us
who carved our self-hatred
onto our skin
onto our psyches
when I wasn't ripping my
soul into shreds
I self-obliterated with black leather
riding crops
fur-lined handcuffs
femmes make the best tops
and I am wound
like tight copper wire
I hadn't planned for sex
to become performance art
I knew that sex was supposed to be
an intimate loving experience
between two people
but how intimate can you be
when you can't stay in your body
when your lover is touching you?
when you are panicked
that they will notice
that your body is there
but no one is home
only to learn how devastating it is
when they don't notice

. . . guess I was a better actress
than I thought I was

Confessional

do you kneel
on cold flagstone floor
when confessing to me
those sins
you longed to keep hidden?
those human failings
dark deeds
fatal flaws
incongruent
with the self-portrait
you handed me
in gilt-edged frame
guileless smile on your face
did you think me
judge and jury
meting out old testament justice?
harsh faced priest
behind the confessional wall
powerful enough
to damn you to hell?
avenging angel?
I do not keep the gods
on speed dial
I am no stone cold bitch
dripping paint brush in hand
ready to paint the letter
of your shame
on your chest
I am sorry
that the lies and omissions
you protected so fiercely
have caught up with you
cracked your beautiful facade

I am sorry
that you are so fearful
that I cannot love your imperfect truth

Depleted

your madness seared through me
unholy alchemy
veins left iron coated
ghostly cells circulate slowly
through this haunted body
that cramps to the floor
shaking hand reaches
for dented chalice
wine mixed with warm blood
ancient spices
returns color to my lips
my tongue

Cat's Tail

word on the street
is cat's got my tongue
but I assure you
that caustic kitty long exhausted
all nine lives with me
it is me biting down hard
with small sharp teeth
feeling the blood well up
behind clenched lips
as I slowly chew up
errant syllables
I long to spit like nails
into the frozen ground
forgive me an angry twitch
or two
of my bottle-brush tail
I am trying so hard
to saunter the high road
with my whiskers pointing north
fighting the instinct
tooth and claw
to swivel my head around
arch my back
and hiss

Cold Bone and Ash

I did not mean
to breathe in your toxic air
studded with accusations
but my gas mask failed
and your cloud of words
penetrated like the discharge
from a shotgun full of metal pellets
unable to discern objective truth
from your self-serving fictions
my lungs are left full to bursting
with particulate gray mist
that I choke on
creating minute tears
in my windpipe
threatening my voice
your casual disregard of my truths
you willingness to exploit my weaknesses
cold bone introduction
of a dagger to my heart
did you mean to muzzle me
like a rabid dog
with shame
with guilt?
you forget that I have mastered
living with the constant bleeding
while breathing in the darkness
and spinning blood and ash into ink
that sears across the parchment

Point of Impact

tiny fractures fan out
like a spider web
from the point of impact
where your thoughtlessly
dismissive words
became an ice pick
that pierced
my glass heart

Unrepentant

shall I fall to my knees
for the sins
you are so quick
to proclaim
I have committed?
you are never satisfied
until my blood paints
the broken glass
and shrapnel
that line your alter
until I fall upon
the holy sword
you are prone to brandish
as you rail at my blaspheme
never one to grant
benefit of the doubt
you self-righteously
rewrite our history
pen yourself the victim
I, of course, the villain
there have only ever
been two choices
for me
in your narrative
savior
or succubae
biding patiently
to suck marrow from
your bones
I should have known
when I tossed my
tarnished halo
at your feet

asked you to see
my truth
not your imagined
creation
we would end up
here again
both of us
feeling wronged
misjudged
betrayed
the collateral damage
surrounding us
littering the
streets

Choke Hold

there is breath
the sharp inhale
of undiluted emotion
that stings
sharp and bright
going down
so much pulverized glass
the slow release
viscous
warm
gritty
thick with double meaning
that I choke on
as I exhale
I try to clear my throat
of you
but you cling to my uvula
resisting my efforts
to expel you
to exorcise your poltergeist
I made you
you rumble angrily
against my vocal chords
perhaps
I concede
as I administer the Heimlich maneuver
viciously on myself
relish the ache of my ribs
as I finally rid myself of you
whiskey chaser burns exquisitely
down my raw throat
purifying me of your taint

Black Widow

donned my
badass black dress
today
mourning colors
for a softer
kinder
woman
I think I used to be
she's fading away
curves lost to angles
all sharp elbows and knees
thorns create a protective trellis
around the bruised petals
of my peony heart
invisible barbed quills sprout
from my death white skin
keep a healthy distance
lest you prick your finger
on my spine
I will greedily drink
your oxygen rich blood
from my cupped hands
before you fall

A Righteous End

I woke in the place
where you play god
naked upon the white
marble sheets
stigmata roses
blooming crimson
in my palms
across my breasts
and sex
a fragrant garland
of my sins
left to adorn
this shrine
the holy spirit
dripped slowly
into my eyes
from where you
impaled me with
the crown
of thorns
you placed
upon my brow
crystallizing the visions
tasted spiced honey
when it fell upon
my torn lips
parched tongue
you roared
blasphemy
accused me
of taking your sacred
name in vain
when I declared

that you were not
my true god
merely an idol
a token
you tried to
baptize me
in the fire
cleanse me
of my affliction
but you are the one
smoldering in a
dark corner
all rage and ashes
while I resurrect
with the dawn
of the sun

Shoes (Charlottesville, Virginia)

my survivor's brain does not try
to process man's inhumanity to man
whole anymore
it scans the image
struggles to make sense of the puzzle pieces
a car
bodies frozen in flight
accidental aerialists
a beautiful tattoo on a contorted back
black truck parked to the right
the horrified and incredulous looks
on the faces of the onlookers
oddly it's the shoes that my mind focuses on
you *really* can be knocked out of your shoes
when a man behind a wheel of car
makes it a weapon
accelerates deliberately
callously
perhaps madly
into a crowd of counter protesters

Magical Thinking

I hide myself behind the hanging coats
praying to a god I already no longer believe in
to turn me chameleon
like the ones I read about
in fourth grade
I plead with the universe
make my pale skin and dark hair
blend in with the parkas
make my left arm plaid
my cheek blue polka dots
make the piled winter boots and sneakers
provide camouflage for corduroyed legs
stockinged feet
cold and wet from melting snow
Please, I beg whatever powers might listen
let his eyes pass over me unseen
let me be invisible to those unblinking eyes
that made me feel so dirty
so naked
just this once

The Name They Call Her

always said with venom
always intended to punish
"how dare you?!" it asked
insinuating that she was uppity
presumptuous
a ball breaker
to draw a circle around her body
loudly declare it '*mine*'
was she 12 the first time
she was called *bitch*?
or was it 16
when she tired of boys
of men
acting like her body was theirs
to look at
comment on
hold down
insult
touch
control?
tired of women
telling her to be
nice
quiet
polite
complacent
a 'good' sport
she was *not* a good sport
rage became a
knife
sharp
deadly
that she learned to yield

much too often
on her own flesh

Young Wolf

politics
sunk our adult friendship
my insistence
black lives matter
collided against
your thin blue line
shower of defensive red sparks
yet you still cross my mind
I remember
15 year old boy
dirty blond hair
spilling over one blue eye
snaggle-tooth smile
crushing hard on another girl
on our island of misfit toys
can't remember when
ground started to shift
on tectonic plates
pushing us onto the same continent
until we were stealing first kisses
in blue twilight
mosquitoes feasting on our legs
seamless transition
from you + I
to us
your hackles raised
police dog on alert
every time *he* was near
didn't need to tell you
you instinctively knew
something was *wrong*
the way he looked at me
talked to me

baited me
punished me
for my rage-filled self-emancipation
in my tweens
sometimes I would still fold up
an origami fortress
after he was gone
a lesser boy
would have trembled
grown man three times his age
puffing out his chest
pissing in the dirt
but you growled deep in your throat
loud enough
long enough
to make it clear
that neither one of us
planned to lie down in supplication
bare our necks to him
thank you for that

Strident

strident
the word reverberates in my mind
I'm not really offended about being called strident
I've been called worse
believe me
'bitch' and I are old, old friends
'fucking dyke' doesn't even raise my eyebrow anymore
my grandmother used to call me 'hard-headed' with
affection
at least
I think that was affection
'strong personality'
came up once or twice in grad school
well, maybe more than once or twice
I guess my classmates didn't know many women's college
graduates
I think it's fascinating that the English language
contains a derogatory word
used almost exclusively
to refer to women who loudly tell their truth

Ode to a Black Eye

I can't remember now
if it was your left eye
or your right
just how puffy it was
almost swollen shut
black and purple
against your pale skin
the white of your eye
hemorrhaged
from the force of the blow

I don't remember
if we asked what
had happened
or if we just knew
I do remember
being in Mrs. Merten's
English class
people whispering
into each other's ears
wondering what you had done
to deserve this black eye
had you pushed John-John
to the limit
flirted with another guy?
been mouthy?
they wondered
a bitch?

you *could* be mouthy
you *could* be a bitch
in the way that
only a teenage

girl can be
I hit you once myself
at a middle school dance
after you said something
cruel and hurtful
pushing a button
that only an old friend
a good friend
knows exists
you just laughed at me
I remember wishing I had
slapped you harder

I watched the swelling
gradually recede
the colors fade to yellow
and green
from my desk in the back
of the classroom
unsettled day after day
that black eye
has haunted me for decades
my silence
has haunted me for decades
I should have told you
that no girl
no woman
ever deserves to be hit
I should have told you
to dump his sorry ass
that he didn't deserve you

but I didn't

it wasn't until

I left our small
blue collar, provincial
Massachusetts hometown
and went to college
that I learned to call
that black eye
exactly what it was

Domestic Violence

Myths Of Girlhood

we were spoiled
for reality
by milk chocolate-coated fairy tales
force fed us
as girls
made to swallow
not spit
myths about beauty
love
sex
taught that only pretty, pretty princesses
could be awoken by
true love's first kiss
impossible standards of beauty
femininity
made for
bitter cherry centers
that left us empty
starving
hollow
how old were we
when we learned
that mere mortal girls
like us
would never be beautiful enough
thin enough
kind enough
pure enough
to win Prince Charming's gold enrobed heart?
we ate up the lessons
that with the right make-up
the right clothes
shoes

handbags
if we took enough quizzes
in *Seventeen* magazine
about how to be popular
how to catch his eye
contorted ourselves into pretzels
we might almost be *enough*
to be invited to dance at the ball
drink a brief taste of
the pink champagne dream
before the clock struck midnight
and we turned back
into pumpkins

Made For Him
Response Poem To Niia's music video '*Made For You*'

she hangs on a hook
suspended animation
not considered alive
real
until he walks into the room
he calls her *doll*
relishes her plastic perfection
the eyes that will never cry
he caresses her once
before brutally meeting his needs
he can unleash his beast
without restraint or care
she is shell with no voice
she cannot protest
complain
she longs to shower when it is over
wash off his stink
her bile
the others surround them
witnesses
trapped in horrified silence
throats without voice boxes
limbs limp
eyes that cannot turn away
they wait for the next man
to size them up
and decide which one of them
is made for him

Objectification

you sharpen your words
into knives
lovingly caressing blade
with whetting stone
until it can split hairs
your goal
to dismember
into assorted parts
a skilled and enthusiastic butcher
you long to reduce women into
arms
legs
feet
hands
breasts
pelvis
head
mouth taped firmly shut
blindfolded
to hide reproach
judgement
in our eyes
to diminish
disempower
silence
how terrified
you must be
of our wombs
our truths
our rage
to think that complete
objectification
nothing short of carving us like

Thanksgiving turkey
can protect you

Stone Angel

I envision myself
alabaster
hard
cold
smooth
immune
to laser gaze
of strangers
that undress me
objectify me
judge me
reduce me
to curves
to openings
they were never invited
to explore
two X chromosomes
sentence me
to a lifetime of eyes
that look
but do not see
words uttered about my body
like a horse being sold
at market
that scratch and burn
like fingernails on the chalkboard
of my psyche
from mouths
that I fantasize sewing shut
with thick black thread
licking the blood dripping
down their vulnerable bare chests
while I undress them callously

with my acid eyes
judge their assets appraisingly
studs for breeding
and observe that they would be so
much handsomer
if they smiled more
if I was not
alabaster

I Knew My Name

I knew my name
when the grown men
called me 'honey'
played with my braids
and pulled my
ten year body
stiff with resistance
onto their hard laps

I knew my name
when the high school teacher
called me "sweetie"
and told me not to worry about
the 70 on my exam because
girls don't need an A in chemistry
to be a good wife and mother

I knew my name
when the teenage boys
called me 'ice queen'
'cock tease'
when I didn't want their
sloppy tongues in my mouth
their rough hands on my budding breasts

I knew my name
when men followed me down the street
called me 'bitch'
'fucking dyke'
when I wouldn't smile
or say thank you
to declarations
of the lewd things

they wanted to do to me

I knew my name
when my children
called me 'mommy'
389 times a day
and all other identities
were lost in a fugue state
of lack of sleep, endless laundry
and dirty diapers

I knew my name
when male eyes
slid off of me like Teflon
as they absently
called me 'ma'am'
after I turned 50
and let my hair turn gray
chiming in that I reminded them
of their mothers
as if it were a compliment

I knew my name
when I finally trusted my eyes
to see my own truth
my voice
to speak it
and rejected those names
I did not choose
I claim my name
And its "Ms. Boss"
To you

Adam's Rib

Adam's rib
aches beneath my breast
titanium splinter
piercing my soul
constantly seeking
to penetrate my self-worth
deliver shame directly
to my bloodstream like a toxin
demands I atone
for eating the forbidden fruit
I still taste the crisp
sweet tart taste
of knowledge on my tongue
and will always
hunger
for more

Jesus Died for Somebody's Sins

Mother Mary
the sinners pray to me
asking me to forgive
their transgressions
their sins
as though I am holy
consecrated by the fire
washed clean in the blood
but Jesus and I never
ran in the same crowd
we didn't pass a bottle of cheap
schnapps while parked in the Catholic cemetery
shooting the shit in a rusty Chevy Nova
making out under small town stars
I never found god in the cardboard wafer
placed upon my tongue
by priests with too-tight white collars
who looked down on me
called me *illegitimate*
offspring of a whore
audacious enough
to marry a divorced Presbyterian
their own vices
alcoholism
adultery
pedophilia
lust
throwing the first stone
gossiped openly about in the parking lot after Mass
do what I say, not as I do hypocrisy
still ringing in my ears as clearly as the *amens*
and *hallelujahs* don't come looking to me
for your absolution

I am no virgin in white
visited by an angel
graced by the god of gods
I was a barefoot wild child
finding the Goddess in the silver light of the moon
the Green Man in the sun-dappled clearings
where I had my first orgasms
fingers dug deep in the earth
ants crawling upon my bare fourteen year old legs
I cannot offer you the grace you seek
only my humanity
my empathy
my deeply flawed soul

Wire in the Blood

the line
between the face
I show the world
and my shadow self
increasingly grows thin
superimposed images
blur
no longer clear
where one ends
and the other begins
I walk
deliberately
heel to toe
on the
knife's edge
between
light and
dark
heaven and
hell
embracing the risk
there is wire in my blood
tang of copper
taste of hot iron
when I lick the rich
red droplets
off my fingers
from the scabs
I deliberately
scratch open
I like how alive I feel
when I bleed
there is purity

to my pain
a high that happy
never offers
I know what I am *supposed*
to want
but my shadow self
wants to drive for a while
that part of me doesn't give a
shit
about content
shadow me craves
tightrope-walk-over-the-abyss recklessness
90-mile-an-hour drives
down winding dirt roads
back alley open-mouthed kisses
in a thunder-storm
there is wire in my blood
and I am the lightning rod

My Sins

I wear my sins openly
black ink tattoos
scrolled over arms
legs
stomach
back
history of the girl I was
the woman I became
I do not lower my eyes
in shame
deference
to your delicate sensibilities
I meet
your questions
judgements
head on
you are not my god
not my priest
the fate of my soul
has never rested
in your hands
keep your pebbles
your stones
away from my house
this sacred temple
I have shattered more than once
re-glued my pieces back together
fractured mosaic of
glass
mirror
copper
steel
do not rest your eyes long

in direct sun
or by full moon
I hear the light
can be blinding

The Skin I'm In

I am not easy in this skin
this ill-fitting suit of normalcy
sags in some places
is too tight in others
it chafes
rubs me raw
soon others will notice
that I am only playing
at human
my demon claws
red eyes
shimmering scales
sharp horns
barely concealed
by this guise
the simmering rage
is starting to blister
the rubbery bottoms of my fake feet
pray there are no witnesses
when the suit bubbles off
in long strips
and truth is revealed

The Monsters Under My Bed

some nights
when I am an insomniac
I lay on the floor
and hang out with the monsters
under my bed
I finally introduced myself
after I tired of them
poking me in the middle of the night
mustered my courage
took a peak

they are quite the motley crew

Vulnerability resembles a giant porcupine
all razor sharp quills
shy gaze
caramel voice
she looks lovely
but it's hard to get close enough
to really tell

Rage looks normal enough
as far as monsters go
but when he gets angry
which is often
his skin gets scaly
his eyes turn red
smoke starts to drift out
from his ears and nostrils
I find myself quite attracted to *Rage*
I want to stroke his reptilian skin
sit close to his heat
inhale his smoke

until my eyes burn red too

Invisibility is pretty quiet
mute actually
not so much invisible
as completely nondescript
I can never remember exactly what
Invisibility looks like
no matter how hard I try to look directly
my eyes slide right off
every time I visit *Invisibility*
it is like meeting for the first time

Memory resembles a ball of tightly wound yarn
pieces of barbed wire and broken glass
protruding out
mixed in with the occasional flower
and seaside picnic
Memory's voice sounds like children laughing
Melissa Etheridge played in the dark
silent screams
heaving sobs
hanging out with *Memory* can be exhausting

Detachment does most of the talking
she wears a sharp suit
pantyhose
sensible pumps
tortoise shell glasses
she carries a laser pointer
used to illustrate her PowerPoints
when I mention that I expected the monsters under my bed
to be *Nightmare*, *Fear*, *Death*
she shakes her head impatiently and tells me that those are
the monsters that haunt *other* people

the ones who only have imagination to rely on
those of us who have looked into the void
seen monsters wearing human faces
are a different story entirely

Hope looks like a sorority girl
on her way to her fifth college reunion
perfect make-up
well-coiffed
just the right amount of accessories
dressed all in pink
tan
well-rested
always smiling
she could be squirting shoppers with perfume at Macy's
she has a bright, breathy voice
always seems to be selling something
like a Club Med vacation in paradise
I don't trust her
not one little bit

Little Me is the smallest
she likes to climb on my lap
hold both my cheeks in her cherub hands
while looking deeply into my eyes
hers are large
ancient
sad
weary
as though she has seen too much
half the time I want to turn away
from those knowing eyes
at others I want to hold her
comfort her
she mostly hums

and sighs
but once she looked at me
and said in her little girl voice
'it wasn't your fault. it was never your fault. . .
it was hard to get back to sleep that night

I mused out loud one night as I grew drowsy
on the carpet
that I wondered which monster under my bed
was scariest
it was suddenly silent
I realized that they were all staring at me
some shocked
some concerned
Detachment pointed her laser pointer directly at my chest
'you, of course
the scariest monster under the bed
is the one you fear you will become'

Wolves

it had been many years
since the wolves
had come and
circled the house
howling at my door
voices insistent
teeth sharp
musk pungent
coats winter thick
and matted

I was not surprised
at their return
it was the full Wolf Moon
I shivered
wrapping myself
in a thick quilt
trying to block out
the mournful
insistent sound

I never knew if they were
demanding retribution
come to tear out my throat
or inviting me to shrug off the last
vestiges of my humanity
run wild with the pack
naked through the snowy night

What Lies Beneath

what lies beneath
this skin
no longer
supple and new
etched with
time's fine lines
that radiate
from tired eyes
faintly shimmering scars
that circle my neck
and pelvis like
ironic smiles
black ink
needled carefully
over time
marking territory
finally and
unequivocally mine?
what lies beneath
these ribs
grown of mineral
laced with steel
that allow blood
to pump
strong and steady
even when memory
bites harsh like frost
against tender fingertips
and toes
and loss sweeps wild
and bitter
crimson tides
down my throat

that try
but fail
to drown me?
the heart of the survivor
beats on

The Choices Before Me

three choices lay before me
rose gold circlet
of willful ignorance
happiness of certainty
guaranteed
never again would I need to question
my words or deeds
indecision
guilt
no longer mine to carry
the diadem of copper poppies
bestowing the blessed gift of forgetting
shoulders lifted
by the erasure of painful memory
brow smoothed
by childlike innocence returned
no shame
no terrors
to haunt my sleep
this tempted me briefly
but I grew worried
that what made me the woman I am
would also be lost
disremembered
the crown of thorns remained
woven of twisted vine
barbs that pierce the skin
it rested most easily upon my head
I was never destined to be queen
writer of truths is the mantle mine
gifted with the sight
my voice a whisper become a roar
pure red blood pricked from my finger

an endless supply of ink

The Alchemist

my past is a dark
ominous cave
that I mine
full of barbed wire
broken glass
rusty metal and
unexploded landmines
I tiptoe carefully barefoot
in tattered rags
through this
treacherous
place
my pain
my rage
becomes the scorching fire
I use to transmute
these dangerous objects
into gem-shaped words
that bury deep into your
consciousness
black diamonds
and rubies
with edges sharp enough
to draw blood

That Which Was Awoken

I had been touched before
knots kneaded loose
from fibers stretched taut
until I flowed
like waves across
crushed shell
this laying of hands
this reverent cradling
awoke things unforeseen
forgotten SNPS
of ancestral memory
knocked loose
from lumbar fluid
bathed me golden
I awoke misty morning angel
stigmata of roses
bleeding from tender palms
lullabies long forgotten
in mother's tongue
spilled forth in fervent whispers
novenas that dispelled the darkness
and banished raw chill
from the bones

This Room Is Not For Rent

the Greek chorus has declared me
damaged beyond repair
incapable of a 'normal' life
'better off dead' say the well-meaning citizens
'than broken'
preferring the image of a golden haired innocent child angel
comforted by a merciful god
over the living angry woman
who refuses to be silent
I try not to let these voices
rent space in my head
they are destructive tenants
who forfeit their security deposit
scrawl graffiti in red lipstick on my walls
dirty
shameful
Lolita
guilty
complicit
whore
bitch
I try not to buy into the vitriol
when they imply that my life has no meaning
that I am an abomination
a red, raw, bleeding thing they deem too unseemly to look at
unfit for polite society
'Fuck You!' I want to shout at the top of my lungs with my hands covering my ears
some days it is hard to find the armor of my rage
when I am so god damned tired
of having to prove over and over again
that I am worthy of continued existence

that I deserve to walk this earth
breathe the oxygen
as if I am the one who must continue to do penance
for others' sins

I Ain't No Damsel

you have mistaken me
for a damsel in distress
waiting for the handsome prince
to come rescue me
slay the dragon
you seem to be under the mistaken impression
that I have no backbone
that previous violations of my boundaries
as a girl child
has left me spineless
voiceless
you appear to be implying
that I am looking
for the right man to come and save me
from my darkness
lead me lovingly into the light
into normalcy
away from the broken thing
you seem to feel I am
you seem to believe that when I write
about *my* sexuality
that this actually has something to do with you

let me set the record straight
I *am* the fucking dragon
I saved myself long ago
I have a steel reinforced spine
a barbed tongue that roars truth
I have learned to love my darkness
I have learned to love my light
I have no desire to hear what inappropriate
unwelcome things

you would like to do to *my* body
last time I checked you are not my lover
my words are not an engraved invitation
into my bed
or the inside of my head
my pen is a flaming sword
and I am not afraid of fire

Resurrection

I rise from the dead beautifully
my gift
self-resurrection
I have brought myself
back to life
a time or two before
inserted the IV
with my own hand
cut through my skin
with my teeth
spread my own ribs
applied the volts
of electricity
directly to my
dead heart
shocked it
until the heartbeat resumed
normal sinus rhythm
before the code
was officially called
body bag lying
unused in the corner
of the sterile examination room
discharged myself
against medical advice
limped down long white hallways with their
unforgiving harsh light
stitches raw
oozing
loosely covered in gauze
walked out
the sliding glass doors
wearing only

a hospital gown
and institutionally issued
non-skid socks
into the waiting night

The Gifts I Am Given

the mirror that I look at myself in
is old
dark
fractured
wavy
distorted
it is as if these glass fragments
have writing scrawled upon them
like so much crimson graffiti
damaged
unclean
fat
old
ugly
bitch
unworthy
invisible
unlovable
objects in this mirror
may be closer than they appear
sometimes they hurt
sometimes they bleed

people have been handing me new words
that they claim they see when they look at me
this language is not congruent
with what my looking glass
likes to venomously spew at me
these are different kinds of words entirely
strong
kind
honest
brave

badass
radiant
beautiful
authentic
powerful
impactful
wise
intelligent
I am not sure what to do
with these foreign objects
I put them in a heart shaped box
for safe keeping
I like to take them out and wonder at them
tracing their curves with my finger

I am thinking about buying
new, clear mirrors
that surround me 360 degrees
and inscribing the glass
with these gifts of words
I have been given
that tell a different narrative of me

or perhaps I will
carve them onto flat disks
of gold, silver and bronze
and string them into a necklace
that I wear close to my heart
it will have weight, heft
serve as an ever present reminder
that mirrors are not always
the holders of my truths

Garden Bed

my ribs
a gilded cage
where seeds of both
my destruction
and salvation
embed themselves
my bloody fingers
a trowel
dig deep into soil
rich in irony and heme
where all things bloom
from the grotesque
to the exquisite
threatening to burst loose
hungry for the light

Gems

sharp edged truths
crystallize in my throat
cut me on faceted edges
as I swallow them hard
with a shot of whiskey
laugh huskily at the irony
of gagging on riches
I long to spit these blood diamonds
rubies
emeralds
into cupped hands
witness the polish they bear
from fire that simmers in my belly
fed on the dry kindling
of a lifetime of suppressed grief
rage
passion
a reckless surgeon
I will slice open my gut
with scalpel
extract them one by one
listen to them ring
as they hit the stainless bowl
before stitching myself back up
perhaps I will use these gems to buy freedom
from the heavy shackles of memory
expectation
that chafe at wrists
ankles
heart
finally unencumbered
I will walk again barefoot
on crisp leaves

a crown of woven branches and
scarlet flowers upon my head

There Will Be Dragons

since childhood
she was told
fairy tales
of brave knights
rescuing helpless maidens
from fearsome dragons
in remote lairs

she was quiet
during these stories
others took this
for fear
timidity
she did not
correct them
she kept her
secrets close

for a dragon
dwelled deep
within her
impenetrable scales
the color of
peacock feathers
fire curling
in its belly
ancient
beautiful
fierce

when threatened
or furious
the skin of

her stomach
her breasts
would begin
to itch
to change
resemble
dragon hide
fire would rise in
her belly
her vision would
change
the world gone red

so far
she had kept
the dragon
contained
held in check
but these were
trying times
her dragon
ached to be set
free

feel the wind
in its wings
roar to the
heavens
show its might
gnash its teeth

she knew
deep down
that she was the dragon
the dragon was her

she pitied those
who meant her harm
or sought to control
the wild beast
within her soul

Nightingale

there are times
when the truths
I hold close to my heart
throw themselves
against the cage of my chest
peck at carved bone and muscle
woven lavender and thorns
they fight to break free
splinter the silence
release nightingale's song
so pure
so haunting
that all that remains
is echoing heartbreak
black feathers & moonlight
piercing the night

Poetry

it is a stir
an ache
rising from my core
growing in urgency
pushing to my surface
gasping hungrily for air
sitting impatiently on my tongue
black pearl
ruby
tear shaped diamond
waiting
for hand to grasp pen
fingers to touch keys
truth to be unleashed
an explosion of my soul
made visible
in black ink

Our Blood into Ink

I reject the stifling silence
I shall speak the hidden truth unflinching
I refuse to smile through gritted teeth
during the rewriting of my history
into palatable bedtime stories for others' comfort
I am finished with these lies of omission
I will no longer be polite
I will not be grateful for tossed crumbs
or patronizing pats on the head
I have no use for pity
I will join hands with my sisters
brothers
warriors all
we shall recite our tales of survival
in clear, resonant voices
rich iron blood shall be transformed into ink
in fountain pens held
by our resolved hands
it will fill page after page
until all our truths have been told
and they blaze brightly across the night sky

Introductions

I am survival
it is etched
on my skin
in black ink
pierced through cartilage &
lobes with silver rings and studs
I am survival
it is knit into
my scalp
under salt & pepper hair
cropped close
when I decided
I was more
than long curly locks
no one's eye candy
I am survival
it is visible
in faint half-moon
scar that circles my throat
& the other that plays
connect-the-dots
between pelvic bones
because square pegs
do not always come out
of round holes &
motherhood is not
for the faint of heart
I am survival
in fine lines that starburst
from corners of my eyes
drawn by laughter &
steely determination
declaring that I am no

mere girl but a woman grown
& I have lived
I am survival
when I clutch my pen
in aching hands
ignoring the pain
in each knuckle
as I cut the silence
in two
with its sharp tip
& refuse to put my truths
back in locked boxes
for other people's comfort
I am. . .

my own

About the Author

Christine E. Ray is a writer, freelance editor, and micropublisher who lives outside of Philadelphia, Pennsylvania. Her writing has been featured in SpillWords, fēlan poetry & visual zine, Nicholas Gagnier's *Swear to Me* (2017) and *All the Lonely People* (2019), *Anthology Volume I: Writings from the Sudden Denouement Literary Collective* (2018) and *We Will Not Be Silenced: The Lived Experience of Sexual Harassment and Sexual Assault Told Powerfully Through Poetry, Prose, Essay, and Art*. Her first book of poetry and prose, *Composition of a Woman*, was published in July of 2018.

An avid writer of fiction and poetry in her teens and 20's, Ray returned to creative writing after a long hiatus in 2016 when she launched her blog *Brave and Reckless*. Although she primarily considers herself a poet, she is best known on WordPress for her well-regarded Series for New Bloggers, which earned a Discover designation by the WordPress Editorial Staff.

She served as primary editor of *Anthology Volume I: Writings from the Sudden Denouement Literary Collective*, *A Sparrow Stirs its Wings* (Rachel Finch), *Blossom and Bone* (Nicole Lyons), *Pantheon* (Eric Syrdal), and *We Will Not Be Silenced: The Lived Experience of Sexual Harassment and Sexual Assault Told Powerfully Through Poetry, Prose, Essay, and Art*.

About Stephen Fuller

Stephen Fuller, also known as SailorPoet, has been writing poetry longer than he has been going to sea, but not longer than his love for the briny depths. He spent many days looking out at the Isles of Shoals imagining, and then he began to write and then he went to sea. Now he is trying to find his way home.

www.ingramcontent.com/pod-product-compliance
Lightning Source LLC
Chambersburg PA
CBHW052051070526
44584CB00017B/2128